The
Scottish
Highlands

Photographs by
Colin Baxter

Text by
Jim Crumley

LOMOND BOOKS

EDINBURGH • SCOTLAND

The Scottish Highlands

It is a world of difference which lies between the Mull of Kintyre in the south-west and Dunnet Head a few miles from John o' Groats in the north. No, it is a world of many differences.

The collective name for that world is the Scottish Highlands, but it is almost as different from the rest of Scotland – whether Island, Lowland or Borders – as it is from the rest of Britain.

The most obvious difference is the terrain, which is mountainous, and low-lying only in its far north-east corner or where it is wedged between the mountains and the coast. It is a land named by the Gaelic language, for the Highlands (along with the Hebrides, but not the Northern Isles of Orkney and Shetland) are the homelands of the Gaels, and the last refuge of their language.

Today's Scotland embraces the Highlands with real pride and affection (although it was not always so) and nowhere on the mainland is Gaelic still the first language. But historically and culturally Highlander and Lowlander have little enough common ground.

Mostly, the Highlands are difficult. Transport is, and always has been, a thorny issue, and the place's isolated distance from both Edinburgh and

LOCH TORRIDON, Wester Ross. The West Highland landscape at its best, with Loch Shieldaig in the distance.

BLAIR CASTLE,
Blair Atholl.
A commanding presence
in the very heart of
Highland Perthshire.

London has long ensured that its needs are at the top of no-one's list of priorities. So in all its civilisations, the Highlands have always fostered a stoical independence among the natives.

The first impression it all makes on today's traveller is of a sparsely populated landscape much given to battening itself down among its mountains in the winter, enlivened only around its coasts, and shedding its characteristic coy demeanour to greet a new tourist season. That is, of course, only partly true, but the remoter fastnesses are much emptier now than they have ever been, for the events of the eighteenth and nineteenth centuries guaranteed that the twentieth century inherited a Highlands at possibly the very lowest ebb in its history, the population at its sparsest.

In 200 devastating years there had been first the hated Act of Union of 1707, which united the Parliaments of Scotland and England and which almost all Scots regarded (and many still do!) as a betrayal by their own kinsmen. There followed the Jacobite rebellion which culminated in the direst of defeats at Culloden Moor in 1746. The London-based Government, then firmly in English hands, set about subduing the troublesome Highlands once and for all, a determination which would

THE RIVER GARRY AT KILLIECRANKIE, PERTHSHIRE

OLDSHOREMORE
A quiet corner of
Sutherland's north-west
coast.

eventually produce the Highland Clearances, and no betrayal of the Highlanders by their own kinsmen was ever more terribly and humiliatingly effective than that. So the twentieth century dawned on a desolate and demoralised place.

Now that we are in the twenty-first century, some old tides have been turned. The Highlands contemplate their future with a degree of justifiable optimism. It has not been that way for a long, long time. It is a good time in the Highlands' fortunes to go and see the butterfly begin to re-emerge from the mountain chrysalis.

As you travel, it is obvious at once that the place harbours another difference. It is, by any standards, very, very beautiful. Furthermore, it is a very rare kind of beauty, for it is composed of two distant strains – the grandest gestures of nature and sea and light, but imbued by the melancholy of the Highlands' human story, by a culture deeply etched and shaded by adversity and exile. There are

INVERNAVER,
Sutherland.

places in the Highlands where the very rocks seem to have absorbed that melancholy, and the beauty of such places is at times all but unbearable.

But the nature of the beauty has also changed, for when the last Ice Age relented 10,000 years ago, the Highlands were quickly colonised by trees, especially birch and pine – that strain of pine which would become the dominant feature of the Caledonian pine forest. In its prime it would have

cloaked all of the Highland glens and many a hill and mountainside up to a natural treeline around 2,000 feet. The howl of the wolf would have been its familiar anthem, and its various eras knew bison, elk, bear, beaver, wild boar, polecat, reindeer and lynx.

Such was the nature of the wilderness which the first tentative humans chanced on 5,000 years ago, flint-users, nomadic herdsmen and grain-scatterers, tiptoeing cautiously out from the Mediterranean up the westernmost fringes of Europe. They came from the north, too, from Norway; and the east, from mainland Europe's North Sea shores. It seems that from the first they established what would become an all-too-familiar pattern of settlement and skirmish. They would interrelate too, the first of many racial unions which would evolve over four millennia into that race of people we now think of as Highland Scots.

A few hundred years before Christ, by which time Bronze Age man had come and gone and been absorbed into the mix of Highlanders, another shadowy tribe arrived, their nature and their origins as unknown as their predecessors, as mysterious as the wondrous buildings they left for every subsequent civilisation to marvel at. What they built were the brochs.

EILEAN NA H-AITEIG
Island of the 'shy maiden', Oldshore Beg, Sutherland.

LOCH LAGGAN,
Badenoch. One of many
long narrow lochs in the
Central Highlands.

The brochs were (the few survivors still are) a phenomenon. They occur nowhere outside Scotland. Their builders are as unknown as their architects. (Yes, architects, for they did not evolve out of something earlier; rather they were thought out meticulously by a sophisticated brain, then built to specifications.) They were tall, up to 60 feet, and they were round. The walls tapered as they rose. They were unwindowed and they were double, never less than nine feet thick but sometimes 19 feet. There were stairs and chambers in the walls and the enclosed circular courtyard was not less than 30 feet wide. There were hundreds all across the northern Highlands, the Northern Isles (where they appear to have originated) and the Western Isles, and a thin scattering in the south of Scotland. Their design never varied.

The broch's heyday lasted for a few centuries either side of the birth of Christ, and its purpose seems to have been wholly defensive. There was one small door, massively barred from within, and no weapon of war has ever been found on a broch site, only artefacts of domesticity. Most were abandoned by AD 600, many dismantled so that the stones might be re-used for other buildings, but even now, their mystique is infectious. Every

LOCH ASSYNT,
Sutherland (opposite),
scattered with remnant
Caledonian pines.

8

GLENFINNAN VIADUCT, WEST HIGHLAND LINE

year, thousands of visitors and students of architecture marvel at the most remarkable survivors in Gleann Beag near Glenelg on the West Highland coast, and at Mousa in Shetland.

The greatest tribute to the broch builders is that they practically defined what would become a Scottish architectural tradition. Every castle for the next thousand years after the brochs fell into disuse still bore their imprint, and so did the humblest cottage, for even these were built double-walled and round-cornered to thwart the sound of the wind.

So the brochs were supremely defensive, but just as mysterious as their origins, was who the builders thought they were defending themselves against. The Romans came, of course, but not till long after the brochs were established, and even then, they made no inroads on the Highlands. The Romans had no appetite for that hostile terrain with its teeming wildlife and its tenacious people. The Battle of Mons Graupius which occurred around AD 90 on the north-east fringes of the Highlands was the one bloody encounter between Romans and Highlanders, and although the natives were overwhelmed, the Romans' days on the Highland edge were already numbered and they withdrew from this most

DORNIE,
Wester Ross.
Well-known to Skye-
bound motorists. The
waters of three lochs meet
here – Loch Alsh, Loch
Duich and Loch Long.

11

LOCH LOMOND
The wooded islands of
Inshcailloch, Torrinch
and Creinch lie in the
southern half of one of
Scotland's best-known
lochs.

unpromising of frontiers to behind a new wall they built between Forth and Clyde. This – the Antonine Wall – they held for a century or two of uneasy peace until out of the fermentation of Highland peoples there emerged a new force. The Romans called them *picti* – the painted people.

The Picts are a great enigma of early Scottish history, for they materialised out of obscurity to dominate the early centuries of Highland history. They have been the source of endless academic argument and the truth, it seems, is no nearer – but they made doughty Highlanders and finally hastened the departure of the Romans forever.

But they were also given to warring among themselves, tribe against tribe, only unifying in the common cause when greater enemies sallied forth to challenge them in their Highland heartlands. In this, they were the forerunners of the clans, and the founding fathers of 'the long brawl of Scottish history'.

They left little behind other than questions. But all down the east from the Northern Isles to Fife they erected standing stones and carved them supremely well. The best of them show skills shrouded by mysteries, imaginative invention whose meaning is lost. It all begs the much repeated

EILEAN DONAN CASTLE, LOCH DUICH

ABERNETHY FOREST, Strathspey, beneath the Cairngorms outlier of Meall a' Buachaille.

question: were such powers of creativity and imagination also compatible with building the brochs?

What finally caused the decline of the Picts was not the incursions of the Britons of Strathclyde or the Angles pressing north out of Northumberland into Berwick and Lothian, but the predatory thrusts of a new threat from across the Irish Seas. It is thought that the name of these invaders was an Irish word meaning 'raider'. If that was the case, it was appropriate enough. The name which the Picts learned to fear came from the Irish kingdom of Dalriada – the Scots.

They began in the fifth century, by raiding among the islands and Argyll, but by the beginning of the sixth century, they had established a hilltop capital on the eminence of Dunadd. Whatever it was which lured them there, it remains a hilltop of almost eerie spirituality. Strange relics are carved into its summit rocks: footprints, a basin, a boar and an inscription in code. It stands above the flat lands of the Moine Mhor – the Great Moss – near Crinan. It is a place from which no fertile imagination emerges unscathed.

The Scots were soon pushing out the frontiers of their second Dalriada, thrusting north and east. Picts, Scots, Britons and Angles were constantly embroiled in minor battles and shifting frontiers, until, in the ninth century, even these diverse foes found a common enemy harrying all their shores – the Vikings.

Finally, that era of conflict seemed to weary of itself. The many truces and intermarriages, the slow spread of Christianity through the Highlands, and the loss of momentum which ultimately afflicts all great conflicts all contributed towards the slow unification of Scot and Pict. In 843, Kenneth MacAlpin became king of both Scots and ultimately the Picts. From that point on, the Pictish culture was snuffed out by the

spread of the Scots who even assumed the Picts' sacred capital of Scone, near Perth.

LOCH AN EILEIN, Rothiemurchus, Cairngorms. The island's ruined castle was once a stronghold of ospreys.

The Vikings meanwhile went ruthlessly among islands and coasts, and made settlements of a kind in Caithness, but their ancient seafaring instincts made little impression on the heartland Highlands. Orkney and Shetland are where the Norse tongue names the landscape we know now. Only in Caithness (where Wick, for example is the Norse *vík*, a bight, and much used in harbour names) did their language hold sway over Gaelic on the mainland. Elsewhere, particularly in the Hebrides, the two co-exist side by side, and there are even hybrid names like Glendale, on Skye, which is the same word in two tongues.

But if the Scots thought that conquest of the Picts would end their times of strife, it was a gravely misplaced belief. In the 200 years between the death of Kenneth MacAlpin and the crowning of Malcolm Canmore in 1057, there were sixteen different kings, and it was during that turbulent era that for the first time a king of England – Aethelstan, a grandson of Alfred – laid a claim to the throne of Scotland.

Malcolm Canmore (*Ceann-mor*, the Gaelic for great head) emerges from

THE THREE SISTERS,
Glencoe. A familiar
landmark to all who
travel through the
Highlands' most
introverting mountain
landscape.

the morass of all that had gone before a clearer-cut figure, and the first to warm ruthlessly to the task of meeting the English threat head-on. By now at least two of his predecessors had bartered away the independence of Scotland, leaving others to buy it back in blood, and the Borders – more or less where they lie today – had become killing fields of a ferocious and sustained slaughter.

It was with Canmore, and particularly his wife Margaret, later St Margaret, that the balance of what we now think of as Scotland began to tilt irrevocably south-eastwards, leaving the Gaelic language and its long Celtic lineage marooned in the mountains and islands.

It is unlikely that much can have changed in the mountain heartland of the Highlands in all this time. By Canmore's time the bear and the bison, the wild ox and the elk had all gone, hunted to extinction presumably, but there are unreliable references to beaver in the West Highlands as late as the sixteenth century, and the wolf, whose demise was scurrilously orchestrated by the hunting classes, lingered wily and elusive until the late eighteenth century.

BIDEAN NAM BIAN,
Glencoe (opposite). The
highest mountain in
Argyll, towering above
Loch Achtriochtan.

So two Scotlands evolved under the house of Canmore – which lasted

CASTLE STALKER, Argyll, looks across to the fertile island of Lismore in Loch Linnhe. It dates from the reign of James IV and was restored in the nineteenth century.

236 years – the Celtic Scotland of the Highlander and the Islander (from which stock Malcolm himself came), and the lowland Scotland whose own rich language came to be called 'Scots' although in truth, the language of the Scots was the one left behind in the mountains.

Margaret was intellectual, cultured and English, and sister to Edgar, England's king-elect. Her marriage may have been his doing, but it was much to the liking of the besotted Malcolm whose brutal regime and bludgeoning of the English borders was tempered by her demeanour and conviction. He even abandoned Gaelic, speaking the language she encouraged everywhere in Lothian, and filled her court with incomers. Her compassion took her out among the poor, where she performed great works. She is commemorated today in St Margaret's Chapel, the oldest building in Edinburgh, high on the Castle skyline. It is a serene room, where an astonishing tradition prevails a thousand years after her death. It is that the St Margaret's Guild – a group of women all called Margaret – see to it that the room is never without flowers.

grave illness, and perhaps of grief for her husband. The double tragedy brought Malcolm's brother Donald Bane out of the mountains to stake a last claim for the Celtic monarchy. It was a disaster and ended when he had his eyes put out by his nephew Edgar and was consigned to a slow death in jail. With Donald Bane, the great Celtic era which dawned in Dalriada was at an end. There would be no more Celtic kings.

Instead, the Highlands grew more and more isolated and the warring kings seemed content to leave things that way, while within the mountains and the islands, the clan system flourished and grew strong and created great leaders of its own.

Clann is the Gaelic word for children. The chieftain was the 'father' of his clan, and his sons or kinsmen would appoint his successor when he died. Loyalties ran deep, loyalty within the clan and loyalty to their traditional lands. But like the Pictish tribes, clan warred with clan, and some of the warring has assumed legendary proportions. The Macleods and the Macdonalds, for example, fought each other all over the islands, and over many centuries. One way or another, and for better and worse, the clan system endured a thousand years before it impaled itself on the

QUEEN'S VIEW,
near Pitlochry,
Perthshire.
Much admired by Queen
Victoria, with Loch
Tummel and the far
profile of Schiehallion.

sword point of Jacobite loyalty — an unfitting end, a doomed enterprise of Highland history.

But it produced a rich culture which still survives. Its most celebrated artefact, and one of modern Scotland's most abiding cliches, was the *piob mhor* — the great pipe, the Highland bagpipes. Clan chiefs numbered hereditary pipers among their office bearers, and slowly, over centuries, pipers ousted the clarsach-playing bard from the clan's cultural hierarchy until by 1700, the bagpipes became the national instrument of Scotland.

There are two kinds of bagpipe music — *ceol beag* (literally the small music) which is slow airs and dance music, and *ceol mor* (the great music) which is the pibroch or classical music, and the stuff of legend. It is worth being in the audience for a maestro of pibroch at least once to see why the Gaels called it *mor*. The old folk will tell you now that the standard of piping and composing pibrochs is not what it was, and how could it be; a player had to study for seven years at the MacCrimmon piping college on Skye to complete his course, and (by the definition of the eighteenth-century pipers) it took seven generations to produce one master player. Times change, the playing of pipe music is not the revered

THE TROSSACHS
Land of wooded hills and lochs on the southern edge of the Highlands, with Loch Katrine in the distance.

LOCH ALSH (opposite), and the distant Cuillin Hills of Skye.

LOCH NESS, Inverness-shire. Lying in the great glen, Loch Ness is 22 miles long and 800 feet deep, and 'home' to Nessie, famed monster. Urquhart Castle lies on its west shore, near Drumnadrochit.

art it once was, but among its connoisseurs it still numbers great players.

The end of the thirteenth century was a dire time in Scotland's fortunes. Claimants to an empty throne bickered endlessly, and no English king of any ambition would stand by and watch so much weak-kneed folly without seizing the moment to press home his own sphere of influence and subjugate Scotland once and for all to England and the English throne. Edward I pressed. He pressed long and hard and he was crafty and ruthless, and he pressed too far. In 1296, he so humiliated a now quite rudderless Scotland, stripping it of its sacred artefacts (including the Stone of Destiny the Dalriada Scots had brought to Scone), that some sort of backlash was almost inevitable. Perhaps he intended it that way. What he could not have foreseen were the consequences, for the backlash was ignited by one William Wallace. Wallace's early life is shrouded in much legend, but whatever single act galvanised him, it propelled him to seek a solution to the country's ills not in what was once Strathclyde (he was the son of a Paisley landowner and descended from the Britons) but in the mountains, where he knew, presumably, that there were still fighting men and free spirits aplenty. First, though, he had gathered about him a small

URQUHART CASTLE AND LOCH NESS

ULLAPOOL,
Wester Ross.
A captivating little
town on Loch Broom,
and ferry terminal for
the Western Isles.

LOCH AWE,
Argyll.

army and killed the English sheriff of Clydesdale in Lanark, and set in motion the Wars of Independence.

The decisive moment came in September 1297, when the narrow wooden bridge across the Forth at Stirling became a focal point long since immortalised in Scottish history. A vast English army floundered here and as it floundered it was butchered and driven clean across the Border. Wallace pronounced himself Guardian of Scotland, a leader by example, possessed of great strength and passionate hatred of the English for the indignities they had heaped on Scotland.

Wallace suffered defeat at Edward's hands near Falkirk the following year, but escaped back to the Highlands. Little is known of his movements until in 1305 he was betrayed, captured, tried in London, hung, drawn and quartered, and his body's pieces displayed around the country by way of example. It was an example which backfired on Edward, for not only had Wallace brought the Highlanders back into the forefront of Scotland's cause, he had prepared a stage on which a more thoughtful leader might unify the country and concentrate its roused fury on a single objective.

That leader was the Earl of Carrick, Robert Bruce. His family had long pursued a claim to the Scottish throne. In 1306, Bruce gathered his followers about him, slew his rival John Comyn the Red in a church, and took the crown. Bruce's early exploits ranged right across Scotland from Galloway to the north-east, and

more than once he had to take to the hills in despair. At his lowest ebb, legend has it, he was inspired by the example of a spider in a cave which eventually triumphed over the adversity of a particularly difficult climb up a web. But legend garnishes Bruce's story the way it has adhered to Wallace's. It is likely that Bruce, having seized the moment in 1306, had spirit enough.

It was at Bannockburn, near Stirling, and within plain sight of the Highland mountains to the north, that on midsummer's day 1314, Robert the Bruce won his immortality. His victory over Edward II's host (Edward I having died an old and worn-out warrior-king seven years before) emphasised his military genius. But it also won Scotland its independence, and peace on Scotland's terms. And as much as such a thing was ever possible, Scotland was a nation united and resolute in defence of its new freedom.

...And the Highlanders went back to their glens...so often, chronicles of the major episodes in Highland history end with these words. For a people which Scotland – and Britain after the Union of the Crowns of 1603 – treated with such disdain between crises, the Highlanders remained

ARDBAN,
Wester Ross.
One of the joys of the
West Highlands is its
shoreline of countless
secret bays, like this one
near Applecross.

25

LOCH GARRY, west of the Great Glen village of Invergarry.

remarkably eager to emerge from the mountain fastness to fight in the name of all manner of causes – king, queen, country, religion, independence from England, union with England. It was always thus for as long as people lived in the glens in numbers. When there was no cause to summon them out of the glens, there were often battles which set clan against clan – Glencoe most tragically, Sheriffmuir most farcically, and most disastrously Culloden, which pitted clan against clan, even brother against brother, in the name of one last great romantic gesture.

Culloden Moor, south of Inverness, 16 April 1746, a high shelf of land above the Moray Firth, turbulent with winds and sleet, the scene of the final throw of the dice for the Young Pretender, Charles Edward Stuart, Bonnie Prince Charlie of a thousand folk songs. That it should all end so ignominiously...yet how he galvanised them! He came from France to lead a rebellion against one more unwelcome dynasty of kings. Rebellion had been in the air ever since the Act of Union which bound the parliaments of Scotland and England together, and like the Union of the Crowns before it, marginalised Scotland in Britain much as the Highlands had long been marginalised in Scotland. Besides, many of the conditions of

LOCH LINNHE
A long inlet of the sea extending south-west from Fort William to the hills of Appin, and down to the Firth of Lorn.

THE RIVER AVON
Rising high in the
Cairngorms, it flows
through Glen Avon and
past Tomintoul on its
way to join the river
Spey.

the Act of Union had been abandoned, and Scotland knew the familiar stench of betrayal in the air.

So Bonnie Prince Charlie lit the fuse of a rebellion which was waiting to happen. He arrived at Arisaig, raised his standard at Glenfinnan, and with only his charm to aid his cause, set about raising an army. But the Government raised Argyll and his Campbells against the rebellion, and that was enough to reawaken the oldest of clan feuds – there were many who had cause to hate Argyll. MacLeans from Mull came, MacGregors from Balquhidder, MacDonalds of many strains including Glencoe, the Stewarts of Appin, the Camerons of Lochiel.

The Highlands would never produce such an army again, and although it never amounted to 10,000 men, and although there were more Highlanders ranged against the Prince than flocking to his standard, here was the spirit of a Wallace or a Bruce in their midst summoning them. Alas, he had neither Wallace's decisiveness nor Bruce's acumen, and after an audacious victory at Prestonpans he tarried in Edinburgh, famously dancing at Holyrood. For five weeks his rebellion stalled, then he stirred again and 6,000 clansmen headed south, and reached Derby. But while Charles wondered what he might wear when he rode into London, his advisers were crying caution. No Englishman had rallied to their cause, and a promised French invasion of the south had not materialised. So Charles turned, and led a baffled and dispirited army back over the Border, and from that point, the last great adventure was doomed. Culloden was a disaster, and in its merciless aftermath, the spirit of the Highlanders was finally broken...and the Highlanders, what was left of them...went back to the glens.

Back in London, the Government was deciding that the Highlanders had been troublesome once too often. They recognised that the removal of

that particular thorn from the flesh of Britain could only be achieved if they nullified the power of the clan chiefs. What sticks in the craw of today's descendants of the clansmen – and all Scots for that matter, now that the Highlands are as wedded to the rest of Scotland as they were once isolated from it – is the manner in which the chieftains were bought by London Government favours. The clan chiefs, so long the champions of their people's interests and their land – their land of all things – evolved, with London's complicity, into landowners.

They took to their redefined role with hideous zeal, and a society in which small parcels of land supported small numbers of cattle was suddenly overwhelmed with sheep, complete with lowland shepherds and estate managers. The calculated effect of all this, to subdue the Highlands once and for all, was unquestionably effective, but in the process it put in place perhaps the darkest of all Highland eras – the Clearances.

It was a simple equation. Sheep were more profitable than the rents paid by crofters. The sheep required the good land to graze, so families were evicted from the good land. Resistance was met with fire and force. The nineteenth century became one long litany of man's inhumanity to man.

BEN LOYAL, Sutherland. One of the shapeliest of all Highland mountains, and one of the most northerly.

THE RIVER SPEY
One of the great rivers of Scotland. Fed by the waters of the western and northern Cairngorms, it nurtures an elite group of Speyside malt whisky distilleries.

THE CAIRNGORM MOUNTAINS
(opposite). An aerial view of its sub-arctic plateau – a National Nature Reserve.

All across the Highlands and in the Hebrides and the Northern Isles, families were cleared by the thousand. Some clung forlornly to scraps of rocky shoreline, but many more were herded into emigrant ships for the Americas and the Antipodes. There, if they arrived alive – many did not – they arrived with nothing.

After the sheep came the deer forests and the Victorian passion for sporting estates. Wealthy landowners acquired huge estates, and fuelled by the novels of Sir Walter Scott and others, the Highlands were awash with romanticism. The Highlander was reduced to a serf on his own land, all the wars in the name of freedom came to nought.

But all tides turn in time, even one as grim as this. A new mood is abroad in today's Highlands, and the seeds of a new regime are being sown. Economics are forcing many landowners to consider selling, and conservation bodies are among the new landowners.

There is a new recognition that an indigenous crofting population is a crucial part of conservation's equation. The opportunity to reclaim a monumental inheritance awaits now that we are in a new century, in a world of many differences which is the Scottish Highlands.

LOCH CLAIR AND LIATHACH, Wester Ross.

BALMORAL CASTLE, Deeside.

People, Communication and Organisations

Second Edition

Desmond W Evans

Prentice Hall

FINANCIAL TIMES

An imprint of **Pearson Education**

Harlow, England • London • New York • Boston • San Francisco • Toronto • Sydney • Singapore • Hong Kong
Tokyo • Seoul • Taipei • New Delhi • Cape Town • Madrid • Mexico City • Amsterdam • Munich • Paris • Milan

Pearson Education Limited
Edinburgh Gate
Harlow
Essex CM20 2JE
England

and Associated Companies throughout the world

Visit us on the World Wide Web at:
http://www.pearsoneduc.com

First published in Great Britain in 1986
Second edition 1990

© Desmond W Evans 1986, 1990

ISBN 0 273 03269 0

British Library Cataloguing in Publication Data
A CIP catalogue record for this book can be obtained from the British Library.

20 19 18 17 16 15
07 06 05 04 03

Printed and bound in Great Britain by Bell & Bain Ltd., Glasgow